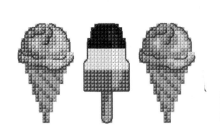

GW00579648

Cross Stitch Motif Series 2

Baby&Kids

400 New Cross Stitch Motifs

Tuva Publishing
www.tuvayayincilik.com

Address Merkez Mah. Cavusbasi Cad. No:71
Cekmekoy / Istanbul 34782 / TURKEY
Tel 9 0216 642 62 62

Cross Stitch Motif Series 2 / Baby & Kids

First Print 2012 / April, Istanbul
Second Print 2012 / November, Istanbul
Third Print 2013 / April, Istanbul
Fourth Print 2014 / October, Istanbul

All Global Copyrights Belongs To
Tuva Tekstil ve Yayıncılık Ltd. Şti.

Content Cross Stitch
Editor in Chief Ayhan DEMİRPEHLİVAN
Project Editor Kader DEMİRPEHLİVAN
Designer Maria DIAZ
Technical Advisor K. Leyla ARAS
Graphic Design Ömer ALP, Büşra ESER
Assistant Kevser BAYRAKÇI

ISBN 978-605-5647-28-5
Printing House
Bilnet Matbaacılık ve Ambalaj San. A.Ş. Dudullu
Organize Sanayi Bölgesi 1. Cadde No:16 - Ümraniye - Istanbul / Turkey

 TuvaYayincilik TuvaPublishing
 TuvaYayincilik TuvaPublishing

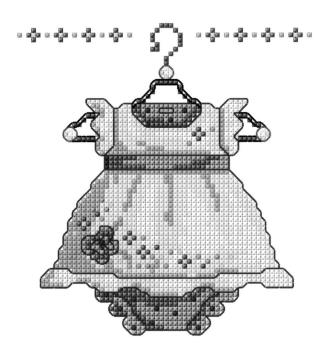

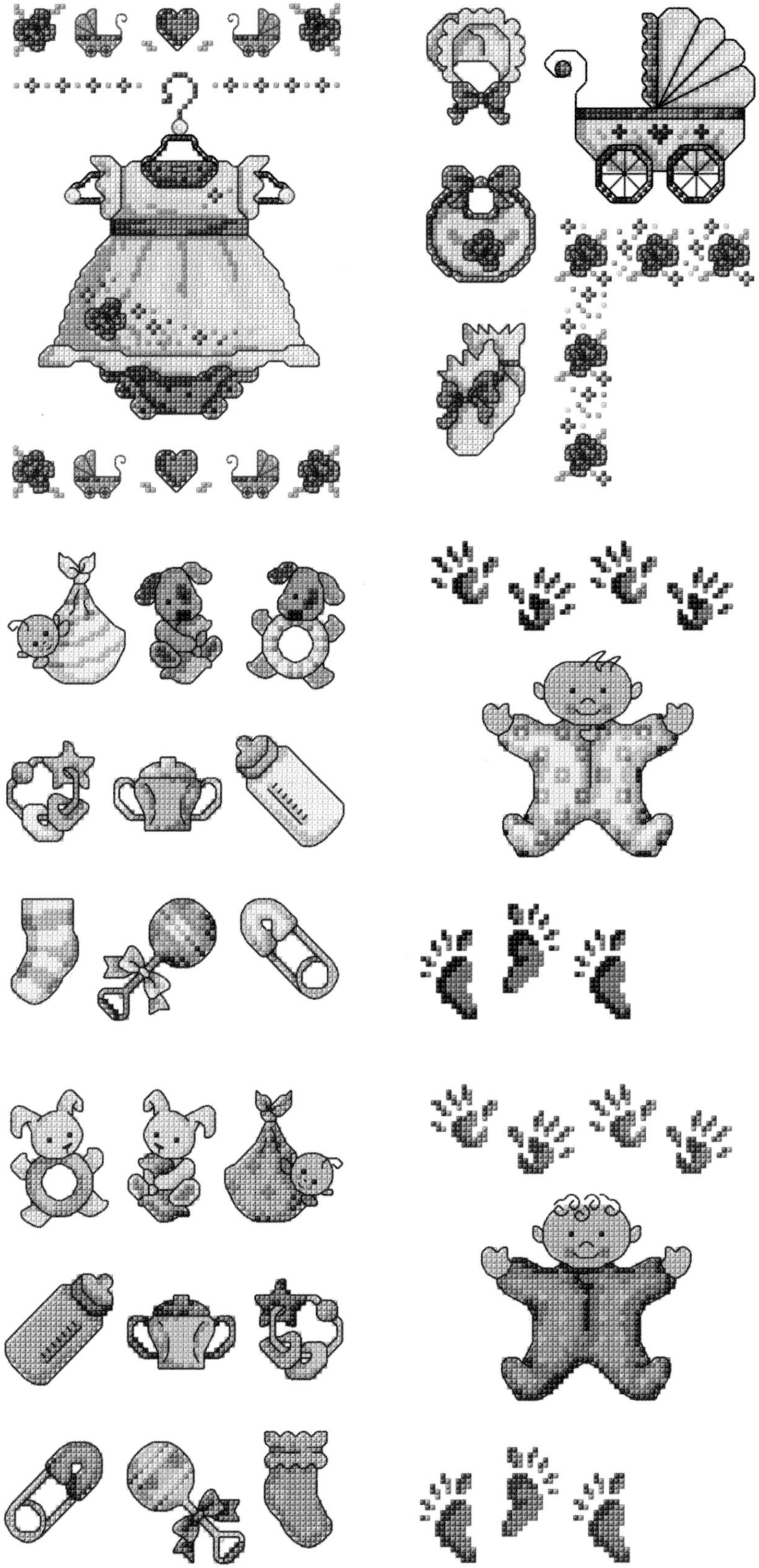

Mouliné
Stranded Cotton Art. 117

U	162
□	435
−	437
↑	726
×	738
+	739
▽	813
F	825
Z	938
O	972
·	3078
╲	825
╲	938
╲	972

□	435
−	437
⧄	601
▽	603
U	605
↑	726
4	702
=	704
×	738
+	739
N	938
O	972
•	3078
╱	702
╱	601
╱	938
╱	972

Mouliné
Stranded Cotton Art. 117

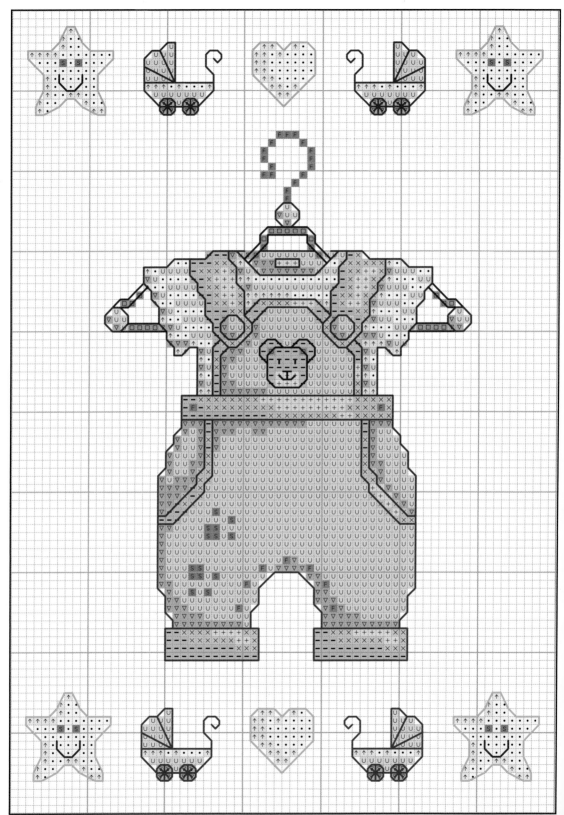

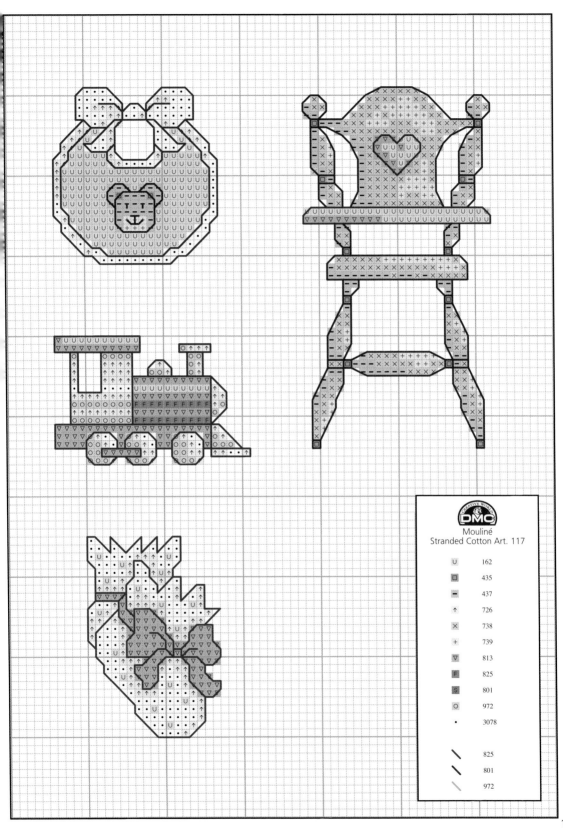

Mouliné
Stranded Cotton Art. 117

U	162
□	435
−	437
↑	726
×	738
+	739
▽	813
F	825
S	801
o	972
·	3078
╲	825
╲	801
╱	972

11

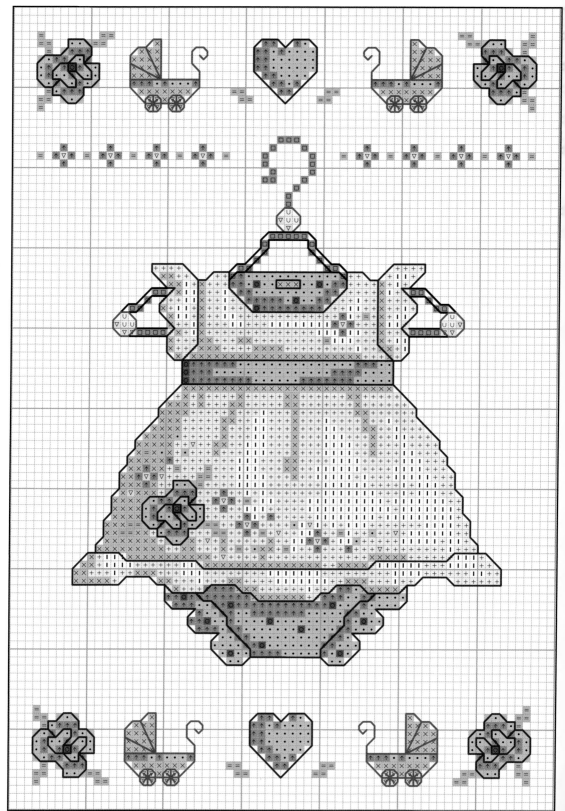

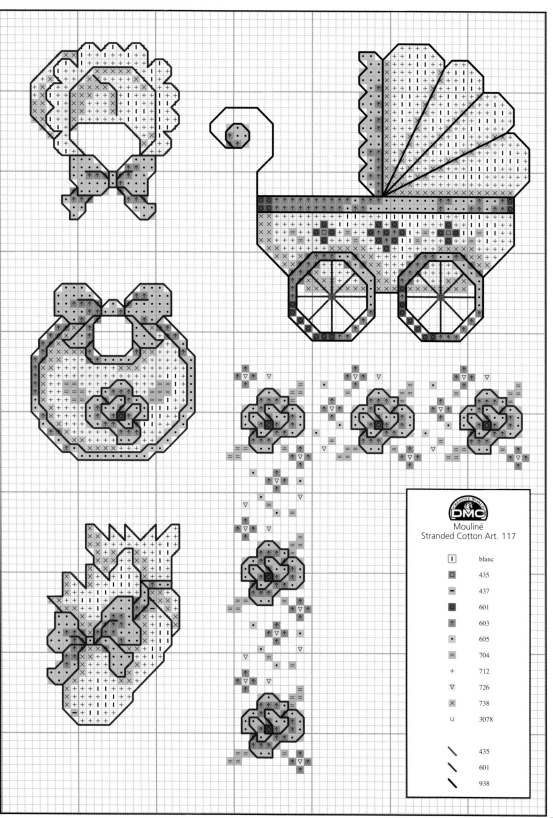

DMC
Mouliné
Stranded Cotton Art. 117

I	blanc
▣	435
−	437
◉	601
↑	603
•	605
=	704
+	712
▽	726
✕	738
U	3078
╱	435
╲	601
╲	938

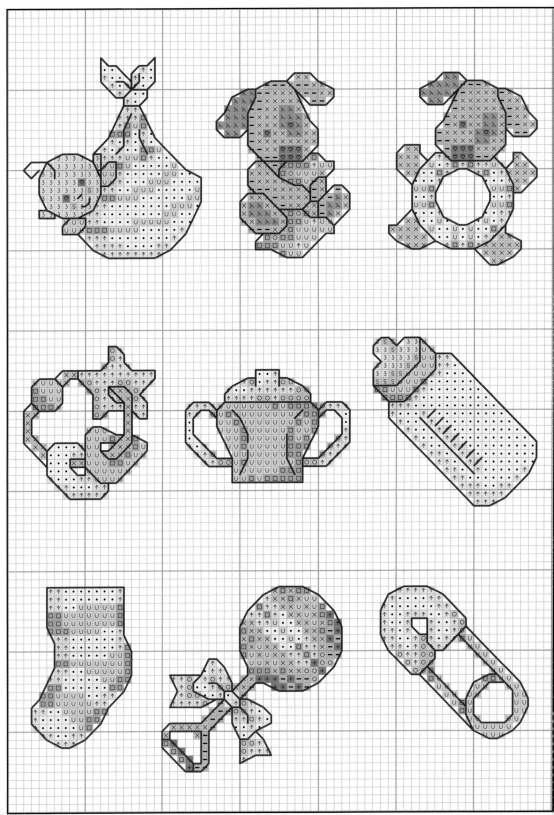

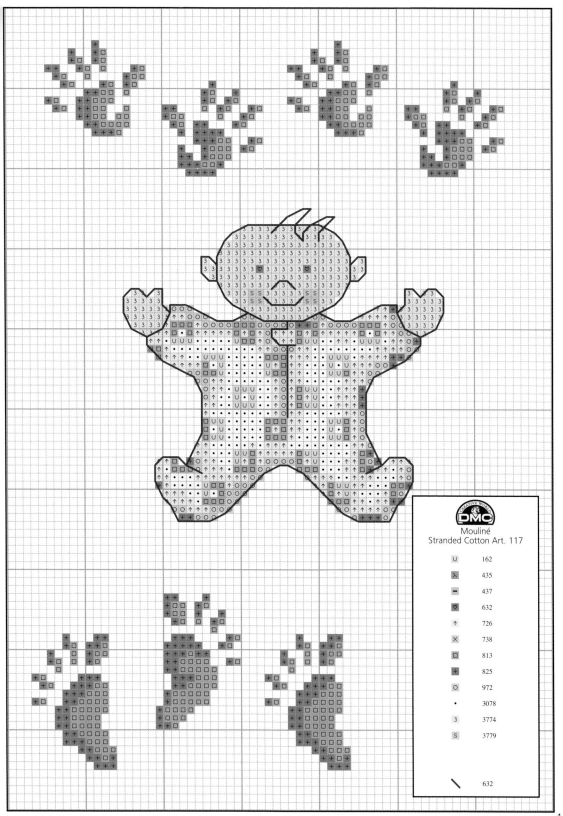

Mouliné
Stranded Cotton Art. 117

Symbol	Colour
U	162
⊠	435
−	437
♥	632
↑	726
✕	738
▢	813
+	825
○	972
•	3078
3	3774
S	3779
╲	632

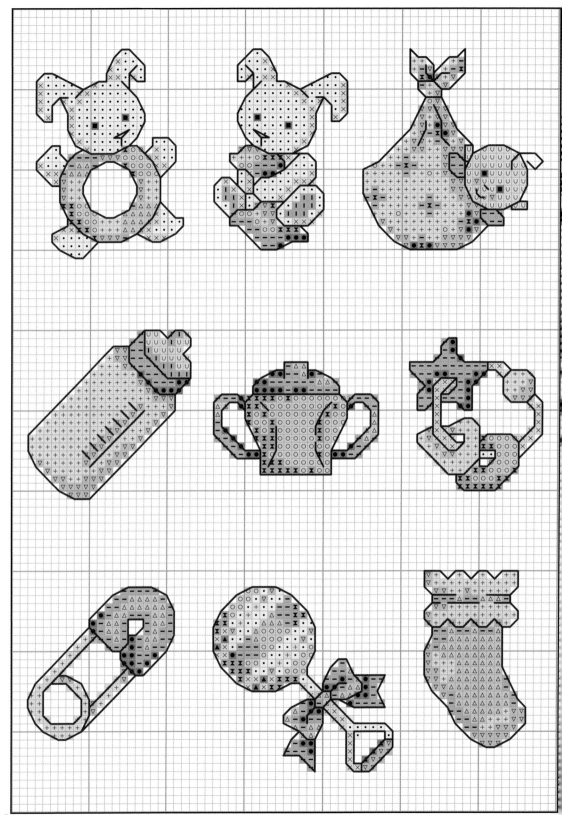

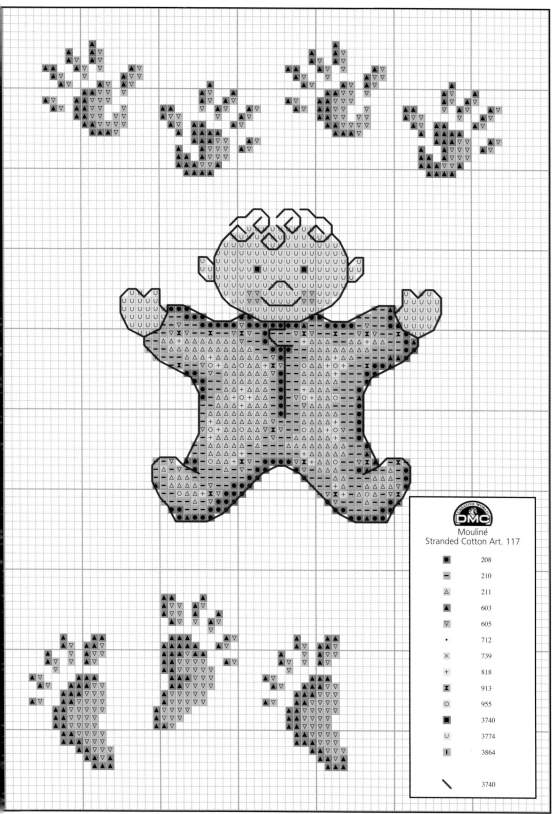

●	208
‒	210
△	211
▲	603
▽	605
•	712
✕	739
+	818
✗	913
O	955
■	3740
U	3774
I	3864
╲	3740

Mouliné
Stranded Cotton Art. 117

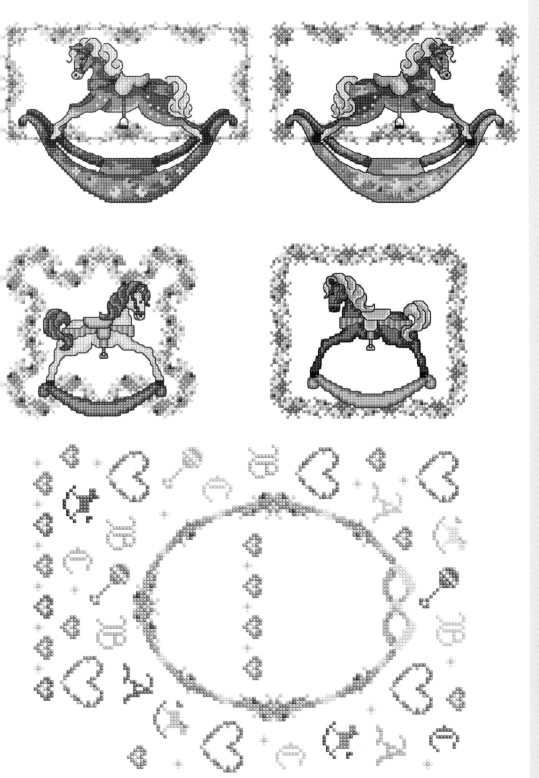

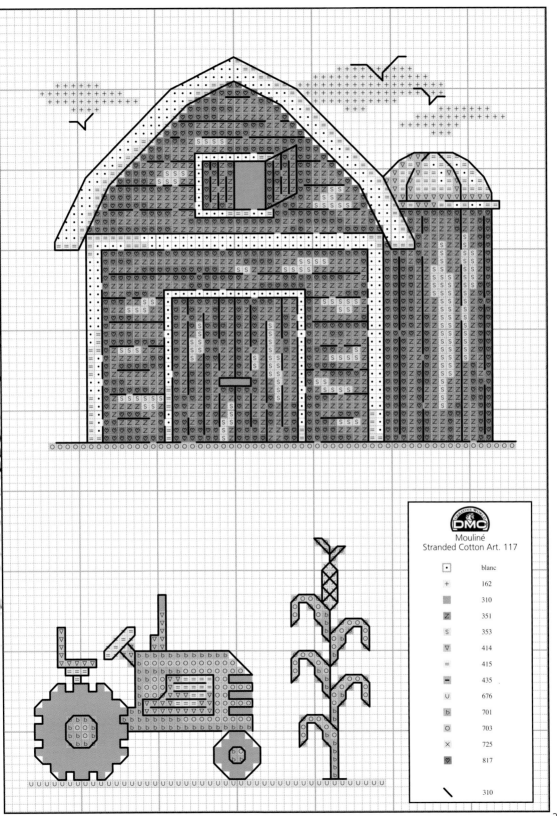

DMC
Mouliné
Stranded Cotton Art. 117

·	blanc
+	162
▨	310
Z	351
S	353
▽	414
=	415
▬	435
U	676
b	701
O	703
×	725
▨	817
\	310

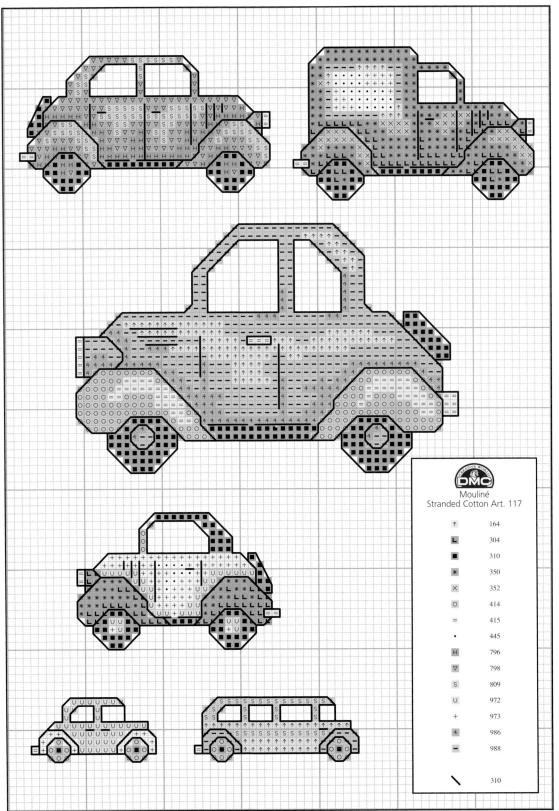

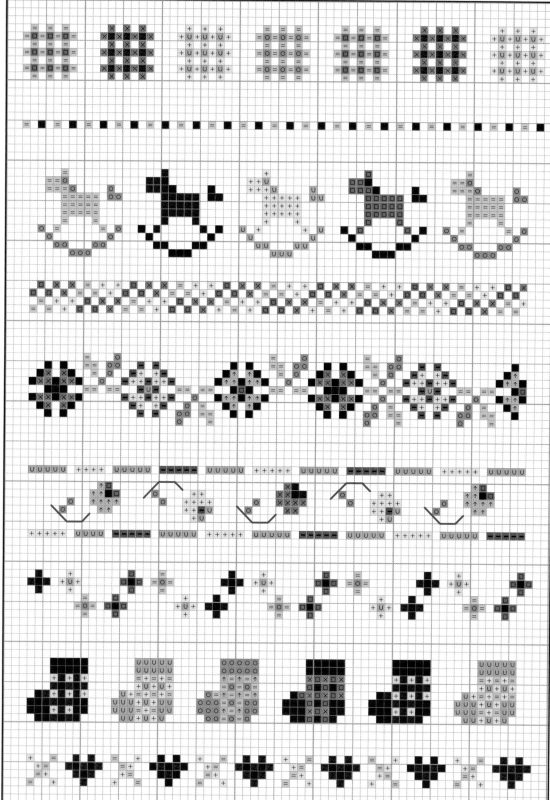

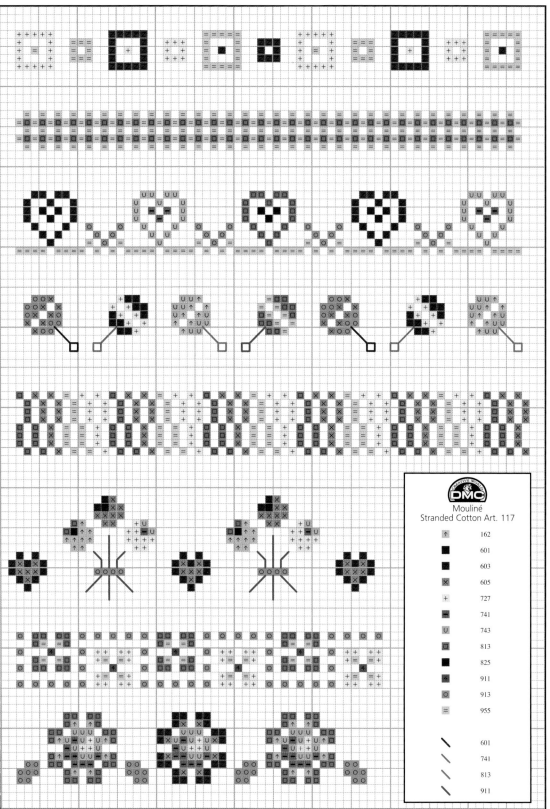

DMC
Mouliné
Stranded Cotton Art. 117

↑	162
■	601
■	603
✕	605
+	727
━	741
U	743
▣	813
■	825
◄	911
○	913
=	955
╲	601
╲	741
╲	813
╲	911

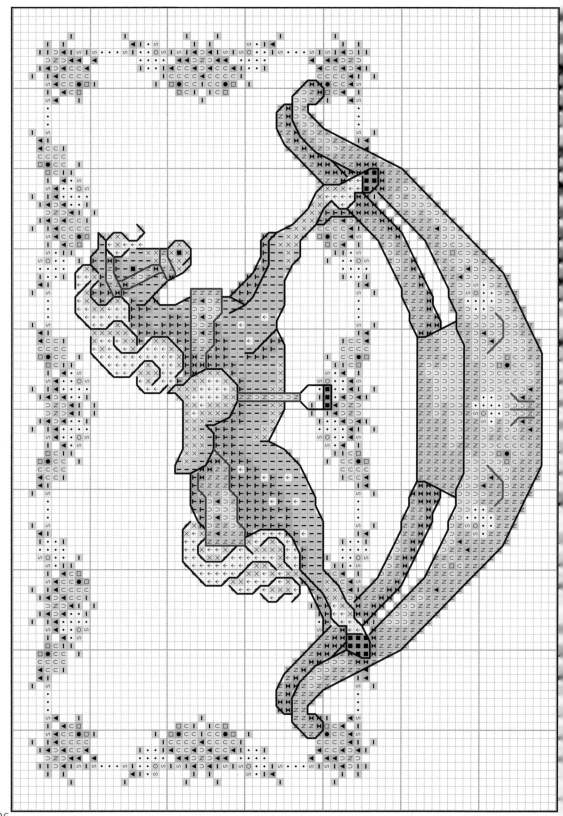

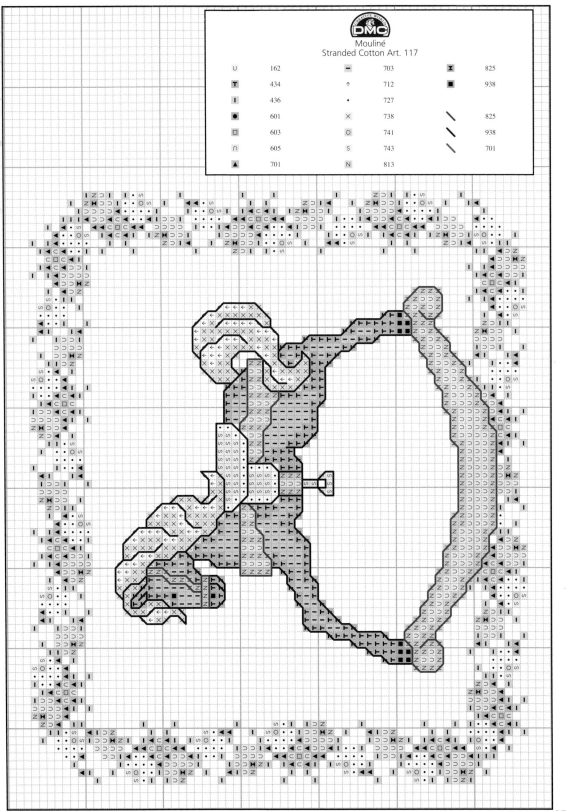

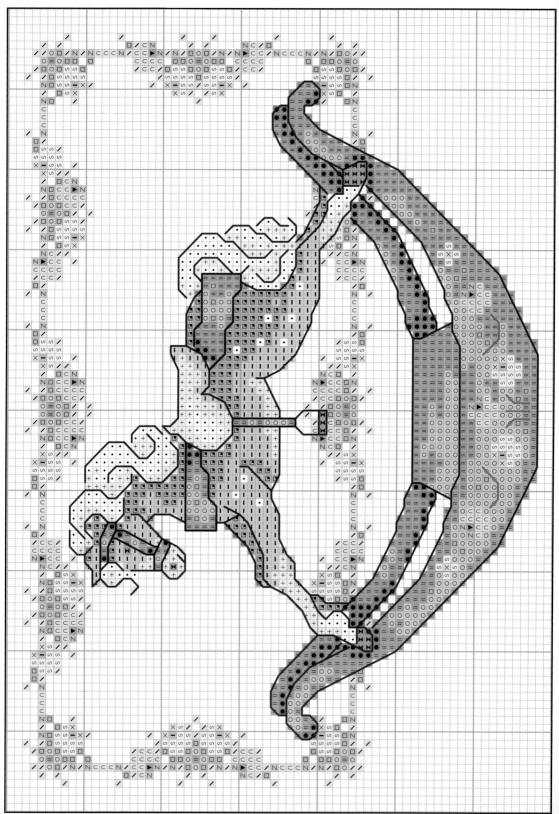

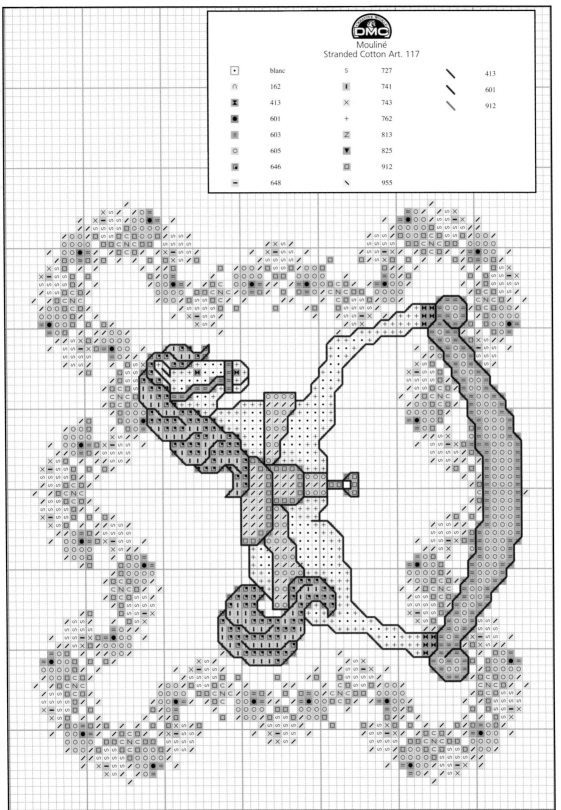

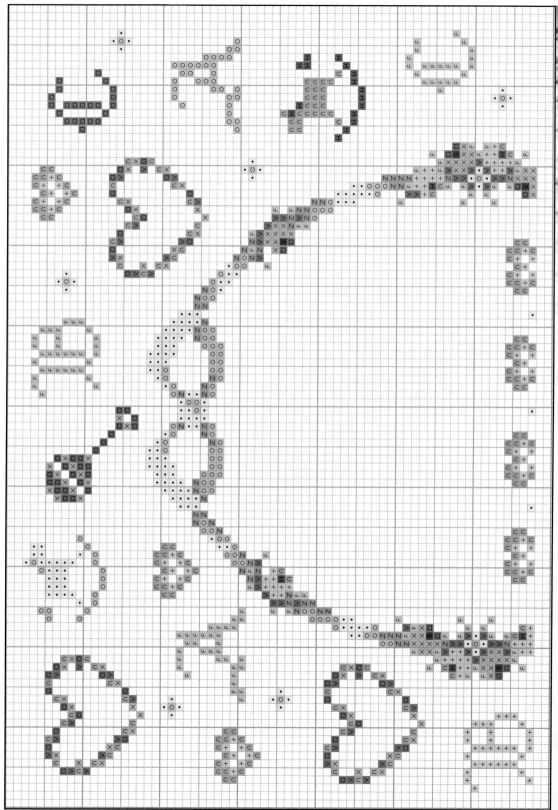

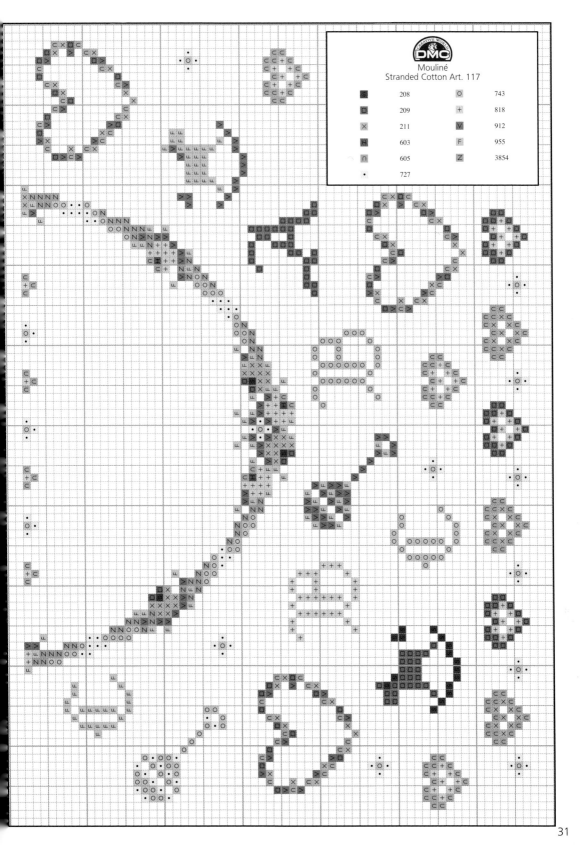

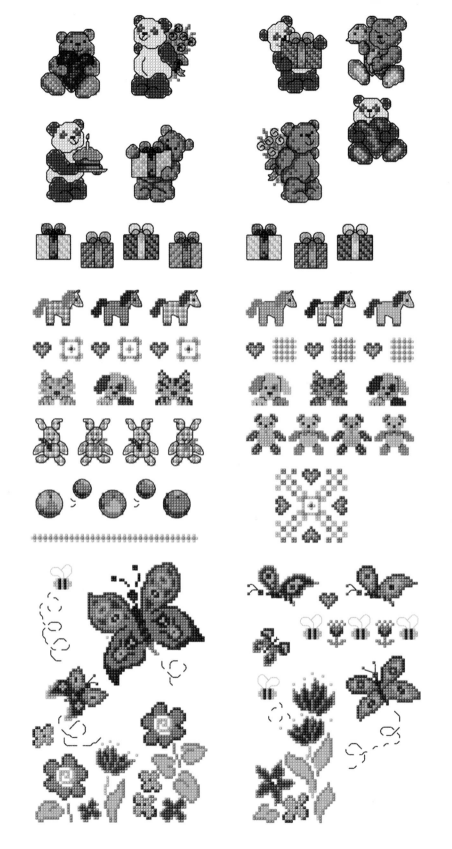

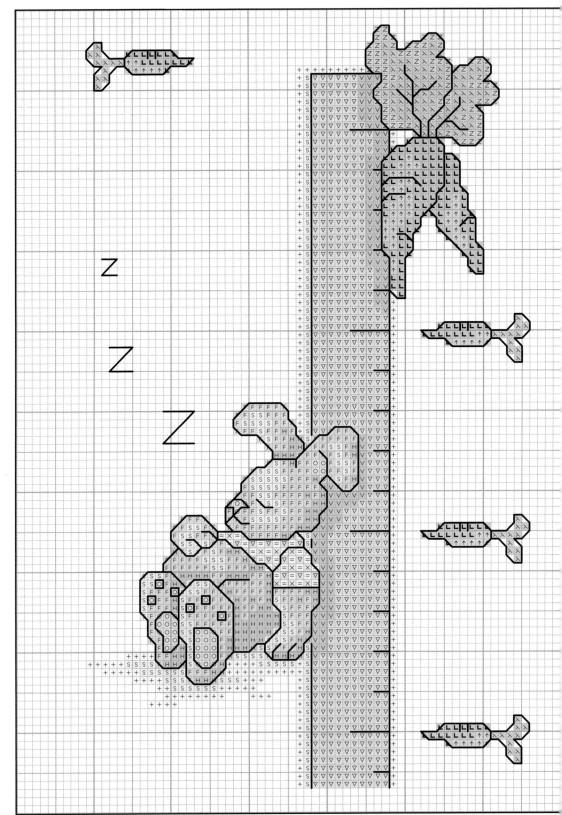

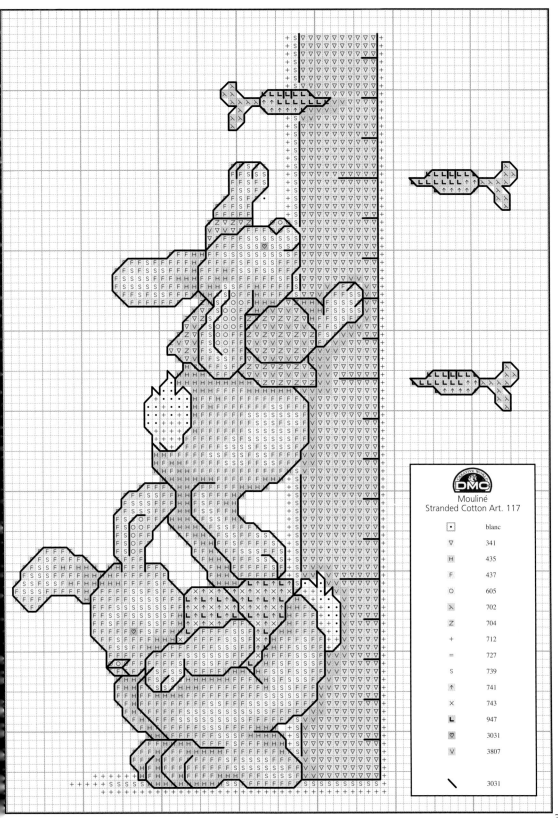

DMC		
Mouliné		
Stranded Cotton Art. 117		
·	blanc	
▽	341	
H	435	
F	437	
O	605	
⤬	702	
Z	704	
+	712	
=	727	
S	739	
↑	741	
✕	743	
L	947	
♡	3031	
V	3807	
＼	3031	

·	blanc
O	162
■	310
⋈	646
T	647
▫	703
+	712
×	727
—	741
△	743
Z	813
●	844
⟍	3033
⟍	310

Mouliné
Stranded Cotton Art. 117

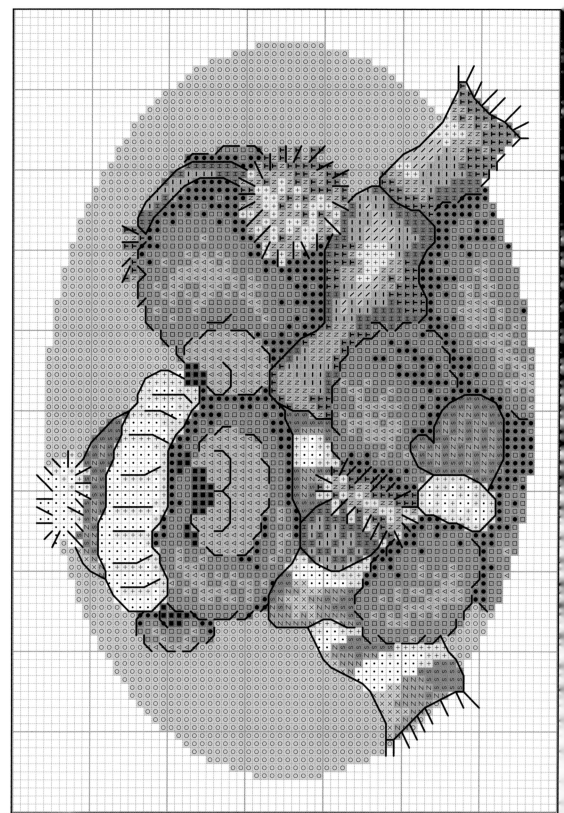

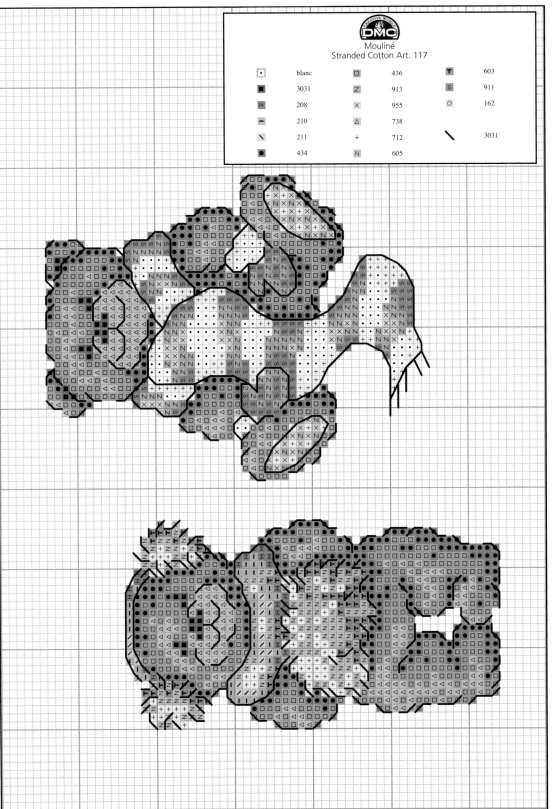

DMC
Mouliné
Stranded Cotton Art. 117

·	blanc	◻	436	T	603		
■	3031	Z	913	S	911		
H	208	✕	955	O	162		
−	210	△	738				
⟍	211	+	712	╲	3031		
●	434	N	605				

	DMC	
	Mouliné	
	Stranded Cotton Art. 117	
·	blanc	
U	162	
N	164	
T	435	
−	437	
▣	601	
Z	603	
O	605	
↑	645	
+	727	
×	743	
I	813	
H	825	
□	988	
■	3031	
＼	3031	

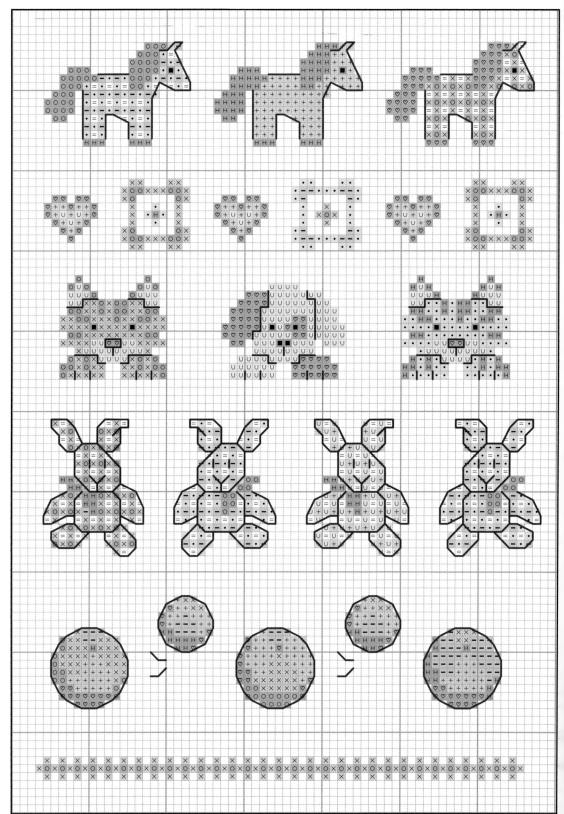

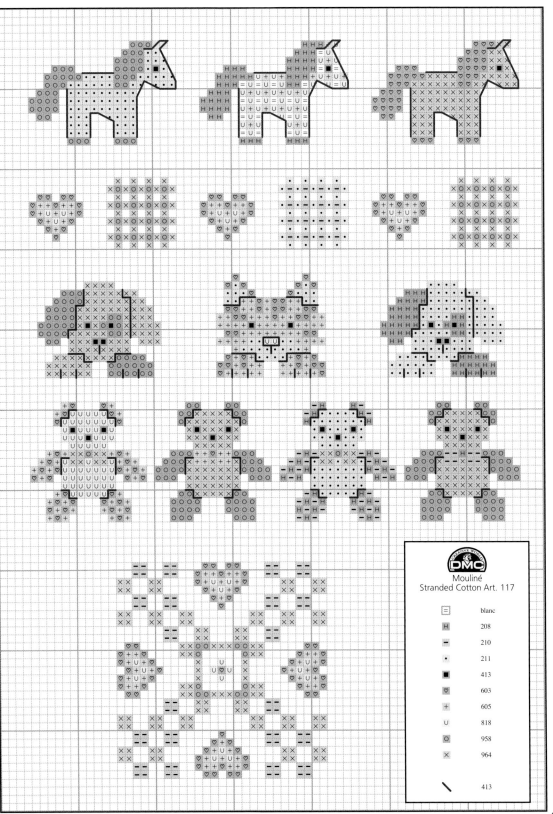

DMC
Mouliné
Stranded Cotton Art. 117

=	blanc
H	208
−	210
•	211
■	413
♡	603
+	605
U	818
O	958
×	964
╲	413

43

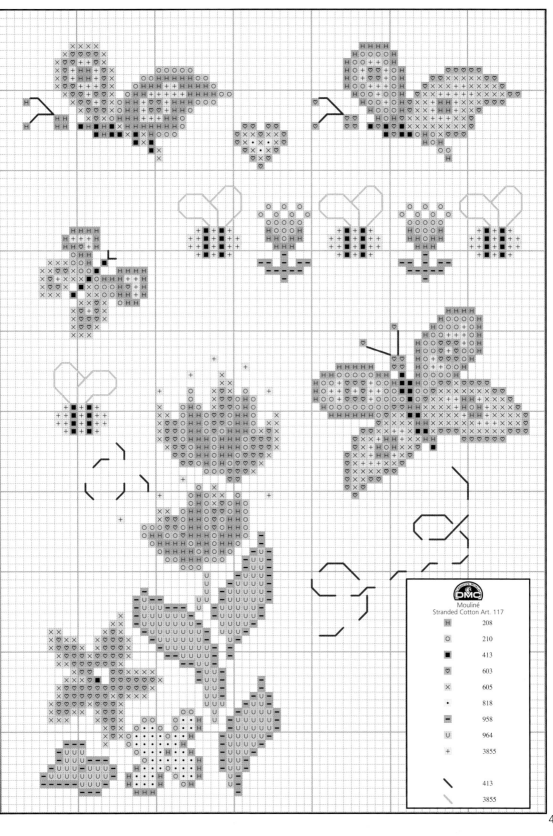

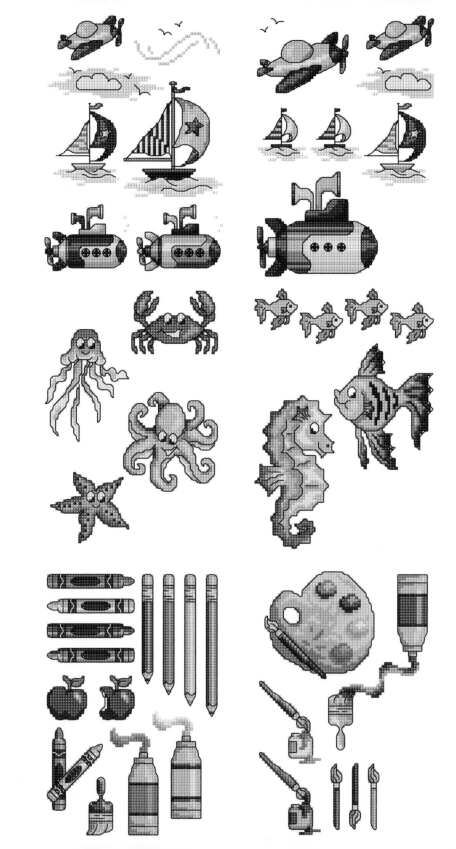

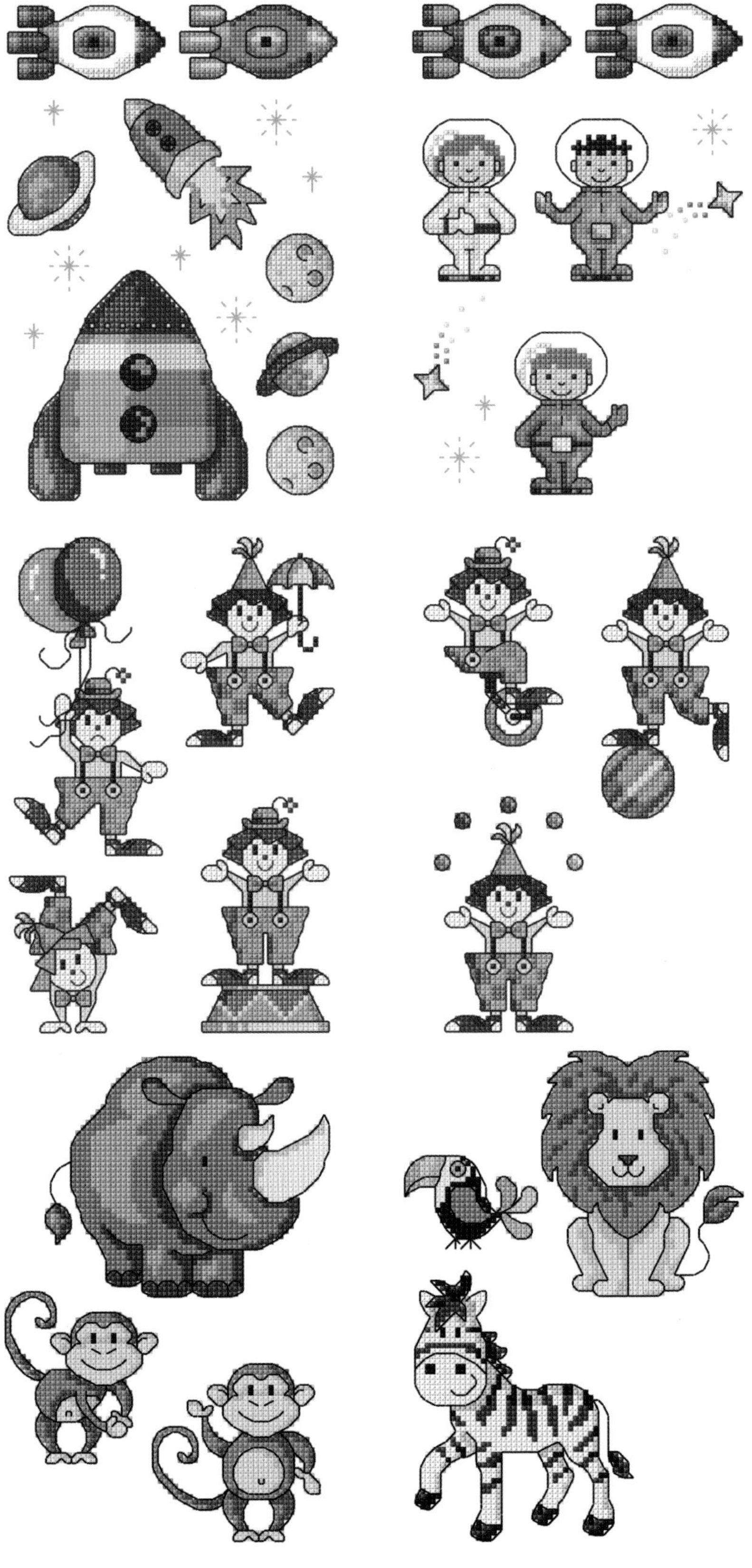

DMC
Mouliné
Stranded Cotton Art. 117

Symbol	Colour
·	blanc
×	162
S	304
H	350
−	352
+	445
△	813
●	825
N	972
○	973
U	3756
■	3799
╲	3799

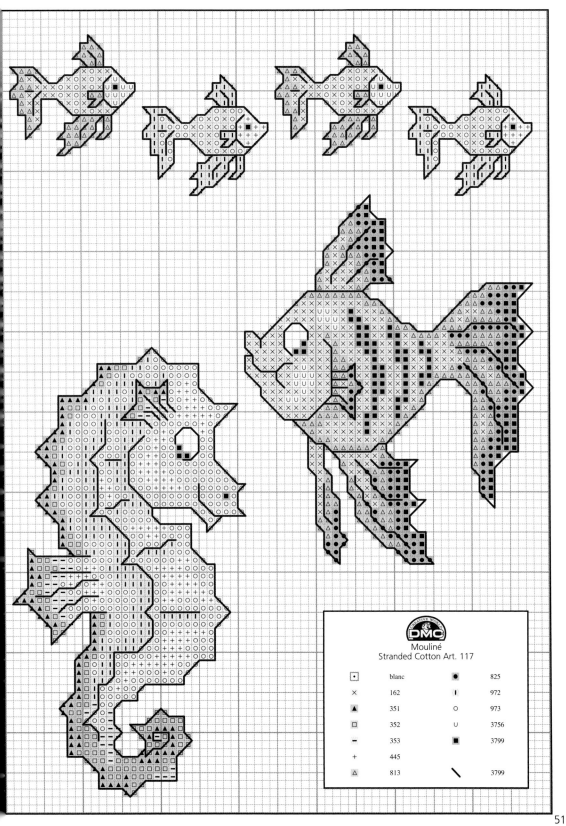

DMC
Mouliné
Stranded Cotton Art. 117

·	blanc	●	825
×	162	I	972
▲	351	○	973
□	352	U	3756
−	353	■	3799
+	445		
△	813	\	3799

51

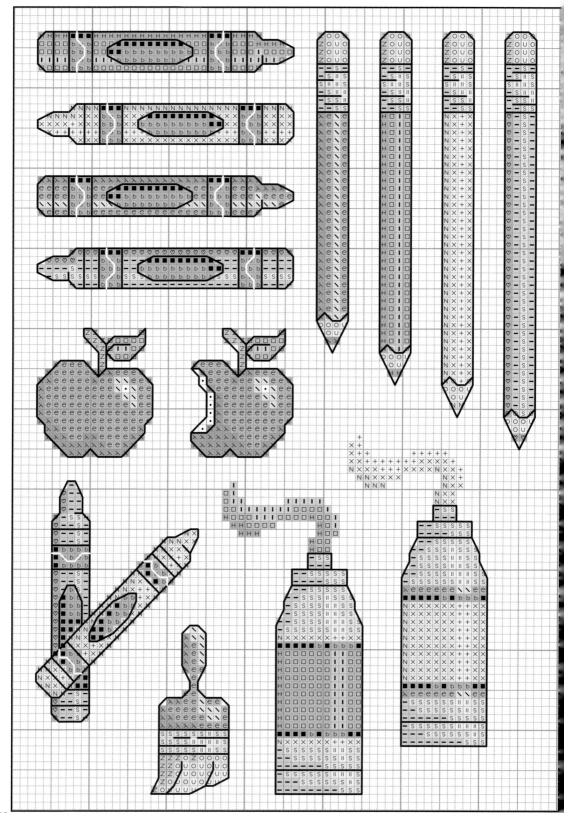

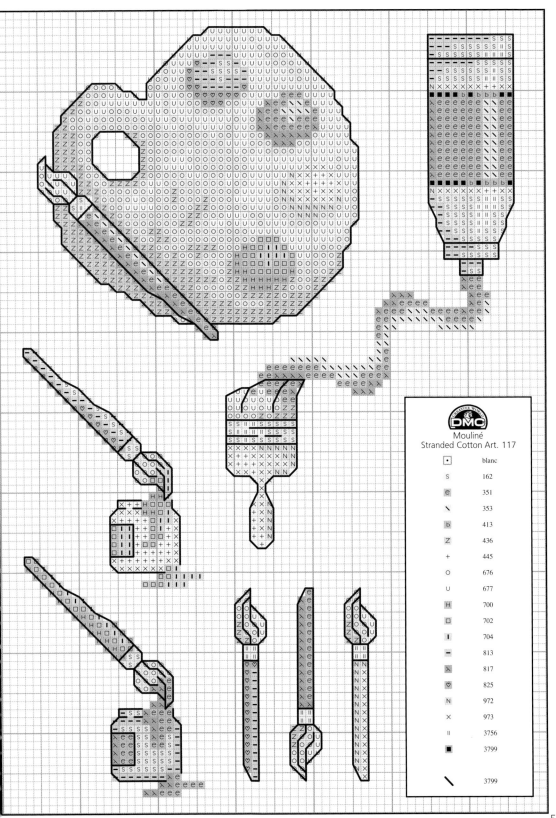

DMC
Mouliné
Stranded Cotton Art. 117

Symbol	Colour
·	blanc
S	162
e	351
\	353
b	413
Z	436
+	445
O	676
U	677
H	700
□	702
I	704
−	813
⊠	817
♡	825
N	972
×	973
‖	3756
■	3799
\	3799

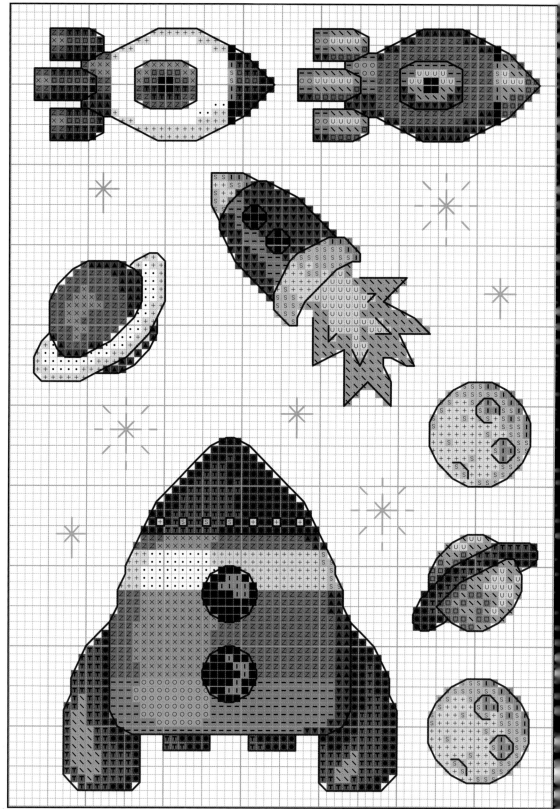

DMC
Mouliné
Stranded Cotton Art. 117

·	blanc
I	318
T	351
S	415
↑	436
×	598
◼	666
▼	701
–	703
▣	740
＼	742
U	744
+	762
Z	807
=	948
▲	3765
◼	3799
O	3819
＼	742
＼	3799

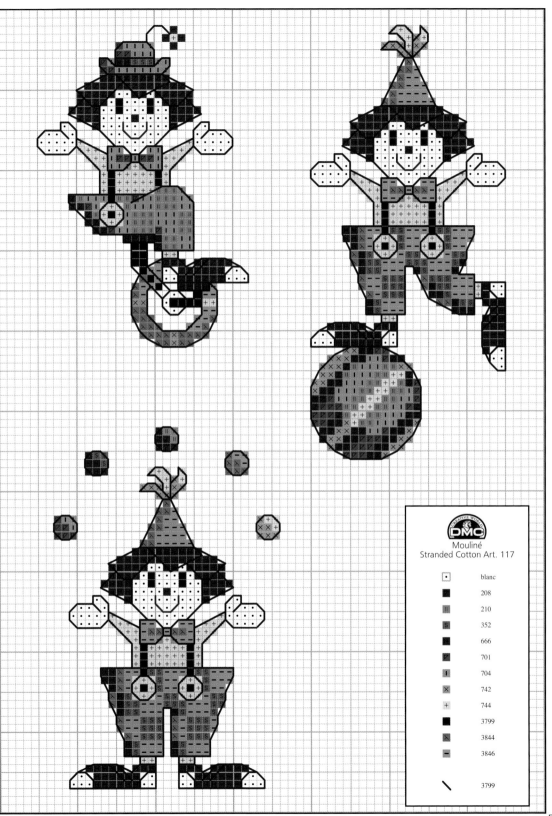

DMC
Mouliné
Stranded Cotton Art. 117

·	blanc
■	208
‖	210
S	352
■	666
▨	701
I	704
×	742
+	744
■	3799
⊠	3844
−	3846
\	3799

DMC
Mouliné
Stranded Cotton Art. 117

▪	blanc
◼	310
✛	341
Z	402
S	434
H	436
◥	605
✕	676
→	677
○	743
=	745
▲	930
◳	3348
I	3747
▣	3839
◥	310

.	blanc
U	165
■	310
9	341
Z	402
H	434
+	436
2	605
×	676
→	677
O	743
=	745
S	930
L	3347
▬	3348
I	3747
↑	3776
□	3839
\	310

Mouliné
Stranded Cotton Art. 117

DMC
Mouliné
Stranded Cotton Art. 117

■	310
▒	434
═	436
◼	666
H	701
\	703
Z	740
U	742
•	744
Z	911
×	913
○	932
+	955
═	3819
\	310

Mouliné
Stranded Cotton Art. 117

■	310
S	434
4	436
⊼	666
N	701
N	703
Z	740
U	742
•	744
Z	911
X	913
O	932
+	955
=	3819
\	310

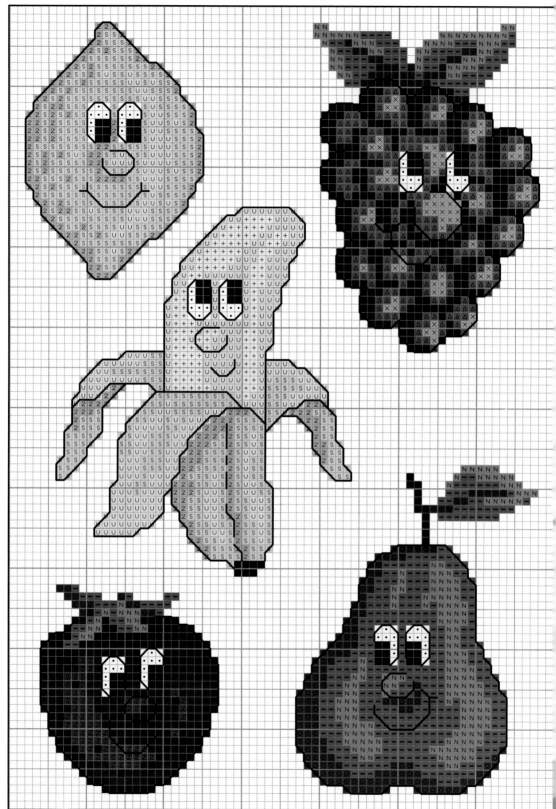

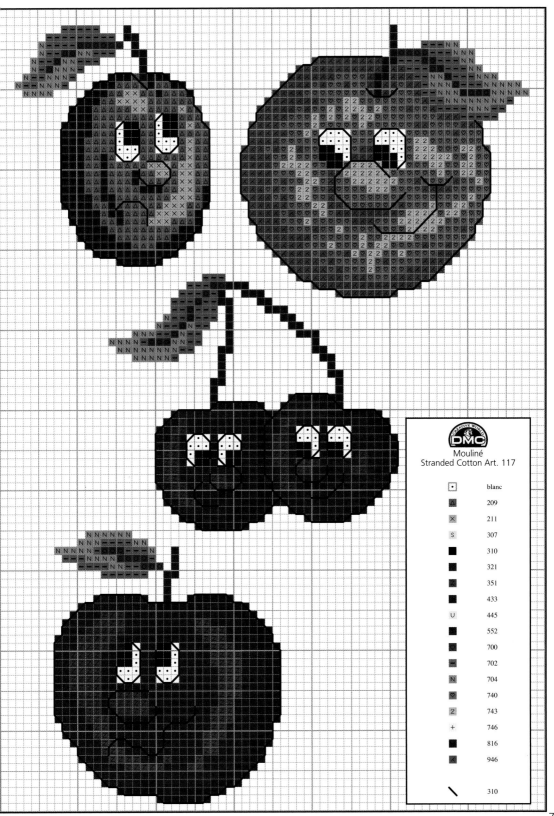

·	blanc
A	209
X	211
S	307
■	310
■	321
■	351
■	433
U	445
■	552
■	700
■	702
N	704
♥	740
2	743
+	746
■	816
✕	946
╲	310

DMC
Mouliné
Stranded Cotton Art. 117

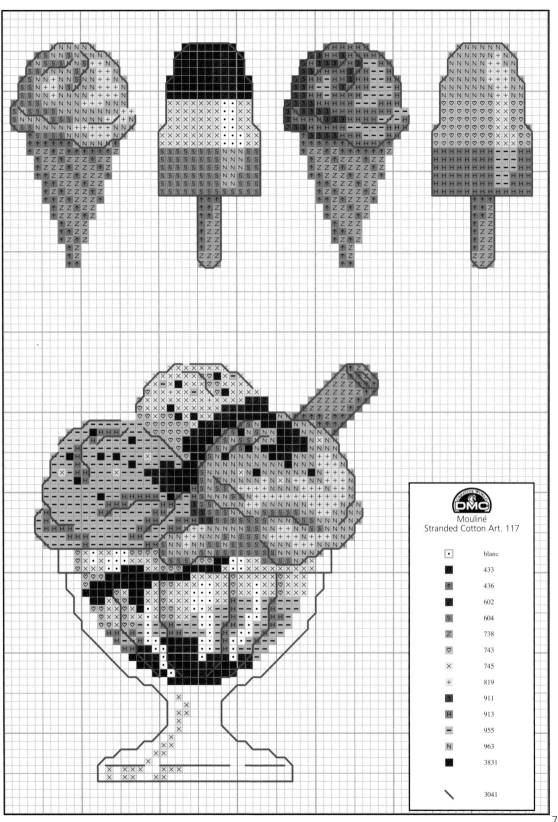

DMC
Mouliné
Stranded Cotton Art. 117

Symbol	Color
·	blanc
■	433
↑	436
Z	602
S	604
Z	738
♡	743
×	745
+	819
3	911
H	913
−	955
N	963
■	3831
\	3041

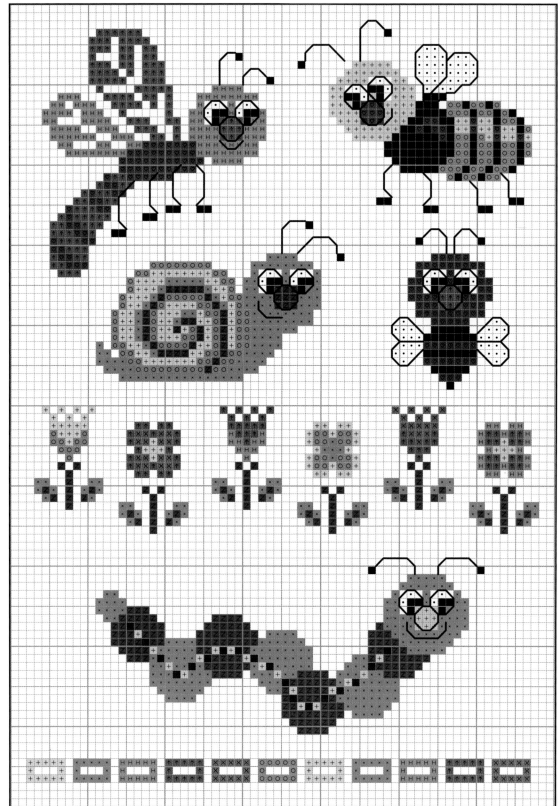

·	blanc
↑	209
+	307
H	341
■	349
2	351
Z	701
×	704
○	742
✕	957
♡	3041
■	3799
╲	3799

Mouliné
Stranded Cotton Art. 117

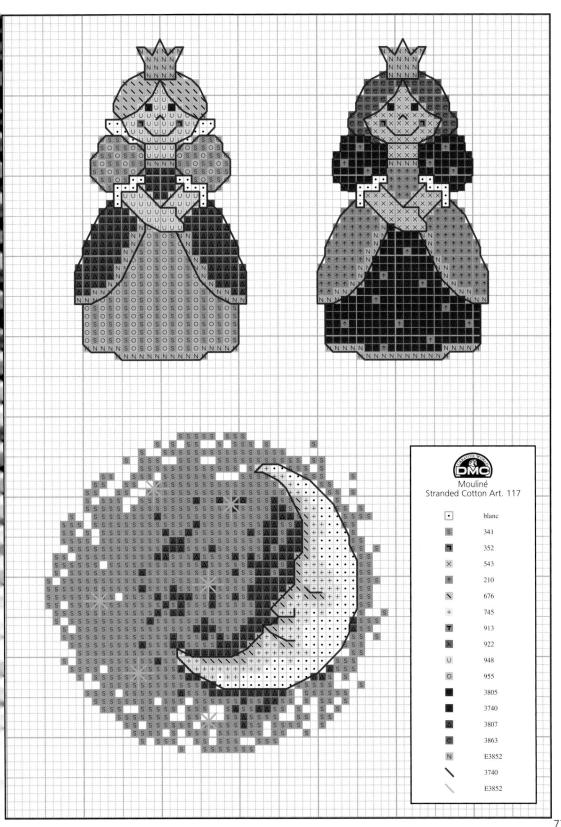

DMC
Mouliné
Stranded Cotton Art. 117

Symbol	Color
•	blanc
S	341
◥	352
×	543
↑	210
\	676
+	745
T	913
✕	922
U	948
O	955
■	3805
■	3740
▲	3807
e	3863
N	E3852
\	3740
\	E3852

DMC
Mouliné
Stranded Cotton Art. 117

■	154
✕	603
Z	704
■	791
S	813
▽	828
↑	963
U	3716
◉	3687
╲	154

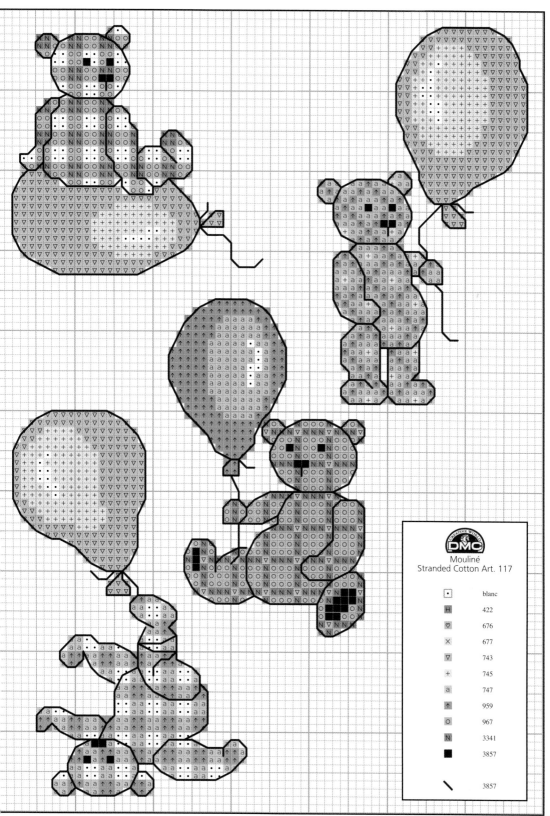

·	blanc
H	422
▽	676
×	677
▽	743
+	745
a	747
↑	959
O	967
N	3341
■	3857
\	3857

Mouliné
Stranded Cotton Art. 117

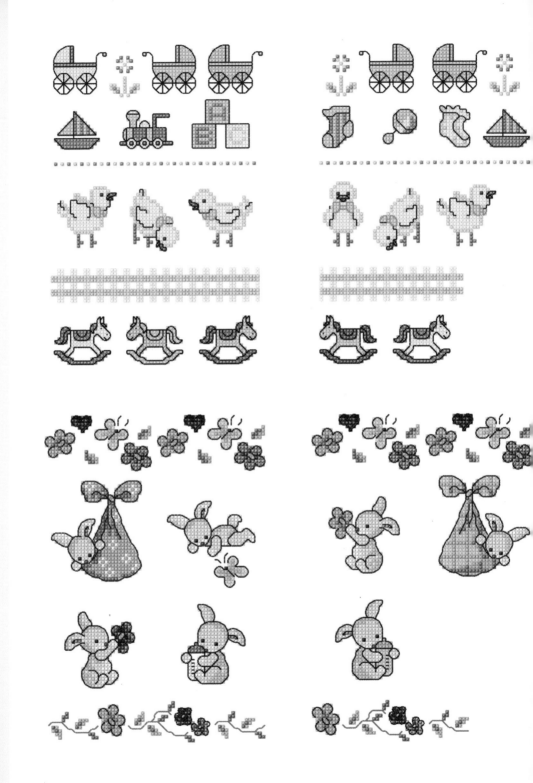

GALLERY 7

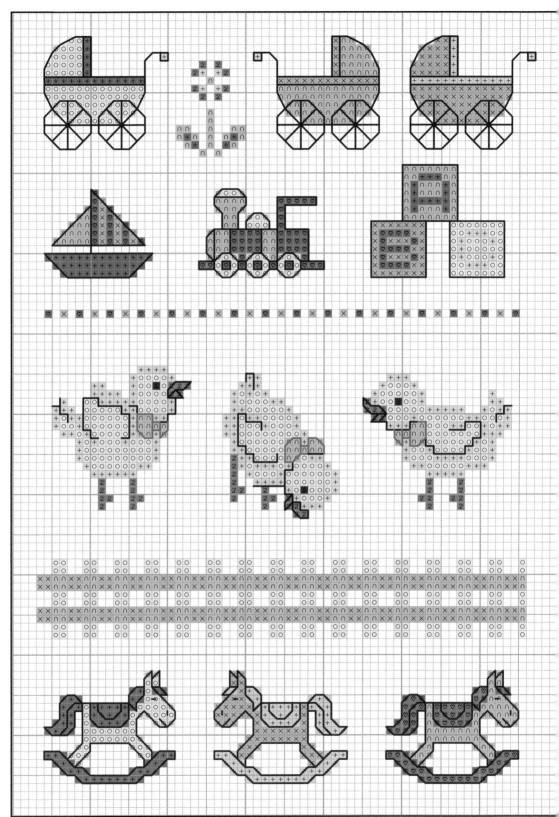

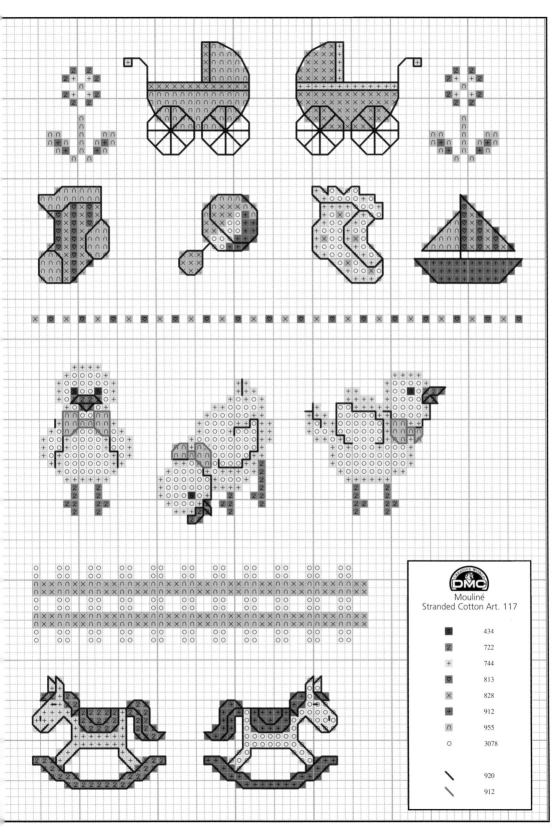

DMC
Mouliné
Stranded Cotton Art. 117

▨	434
2	722
+	744
♥	813
✕	828
▥	912
∩	955
○	3078
╱	920
╱	912

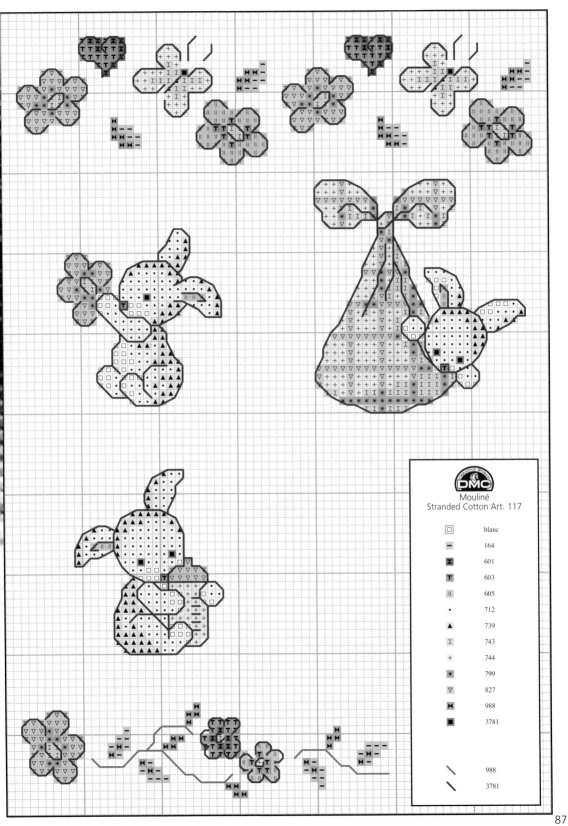

□	blanc
−	164
✖	601
T	603
‖	605
•	712
▲	739
I	743
+	744
✳	799
▽	827
⋈	988
■	3781
╲	988
╲	3781

Mouliné
Stranded Cotton Art. 117

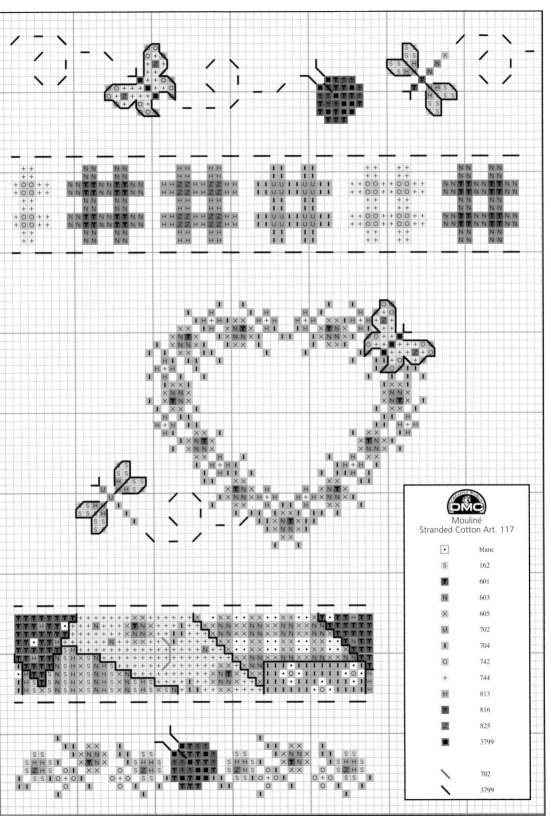

DMC
Mouliné
Stranded Cotton Art. 117

·	blanc	
S	162	
T	601	
N	603	
X	605	
U	702	
I	704	
O	742	
+	744	
H	813	
▨	816	
Z	825	
■	3799	
╱	702	
╲	3799	

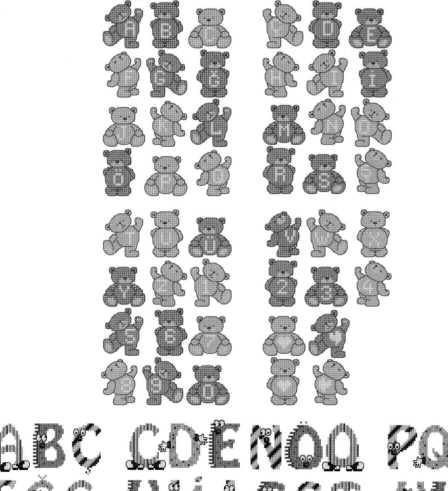

AaBbCcÇçDdEe
FfGğĞğHhIıİiJj
KkLlMmNnOo
ÖöPpQqRrSsŞş
TtUuÜüVvWw
XxYyZz

ABCÇDEFGĞHIİJK
LMNOÖPQRSŞTUÜ
VWXYZ 0123456789

AaBbCcÇçDdEe
FfGgĞğHhIıİiJj
KkLlMmNnOoÖö
PpQqRrSsŞşTt
UuÜüVvW
wXxYyZz

Aa Bb Cc Çç Dd Ee Ff Gg
Gğ Hh Iı İi Jj Kk Ll Mm Nn
Oo Öö Pp Qq Rr Ss Şş Tt
Uu Üü Vv Ww Xx Yy Zz

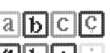 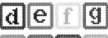   

CÇDEFGĞHIİ
JKLMNOÖPQR
ŞSTUÜVWYZ
1234567890

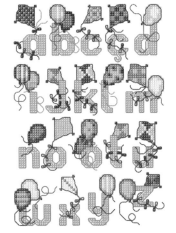 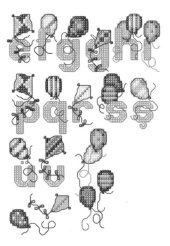

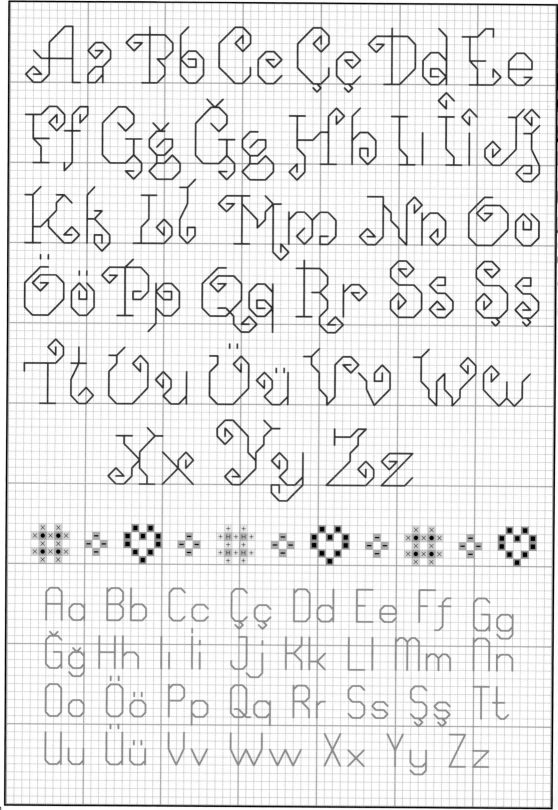

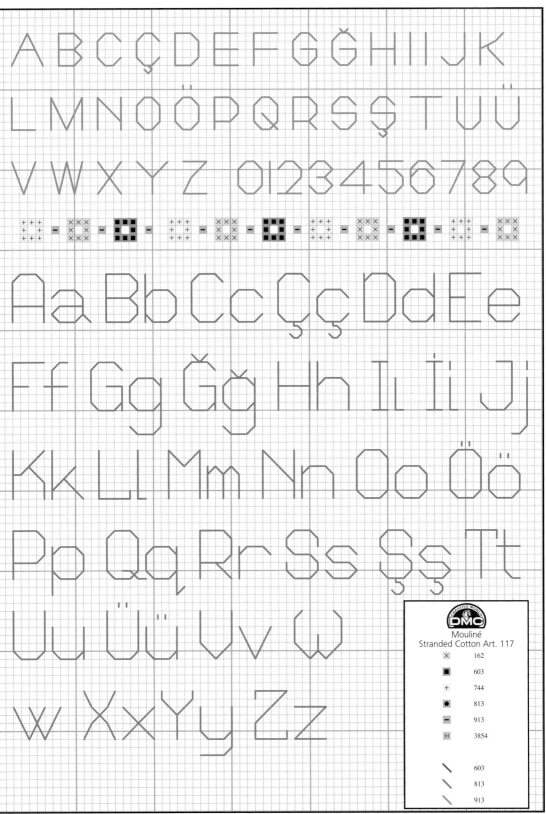

ABCÇDEFGGĞHIİJK
LMNOÖPQRSŞTUÜ
VWXYZ0123456789

AaBbCcÇçDdEe
FfGgĞğHhIıİiJj
KkLlMmNnOoÖö
PpQqRrSsŞşTt
UuÜüVvWw
WXxYyZz

DMC
Mouliné
Stranded Cotton Art. 117

×	162
■	603
+	744
●	813
–	913
H	3854
╲	603
╲	813
╱	913

DMC
Mouliné
Stranded Cotton Art. 117

–	966
✕	437
•	712
+	739
T	3716
○	3841
◼	3862
◼	3862
╲	3862

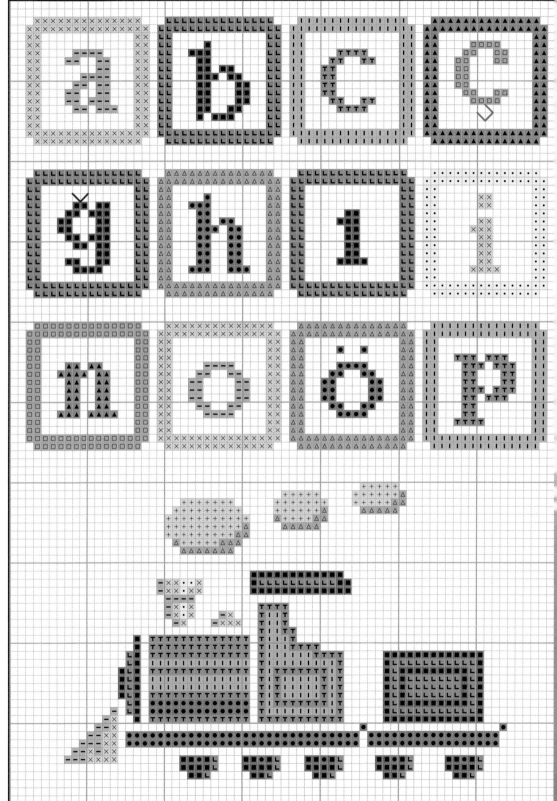

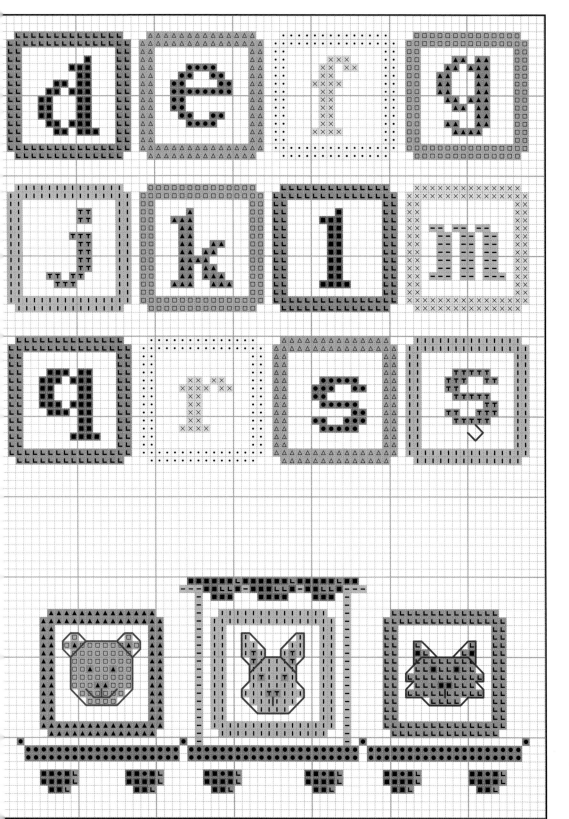

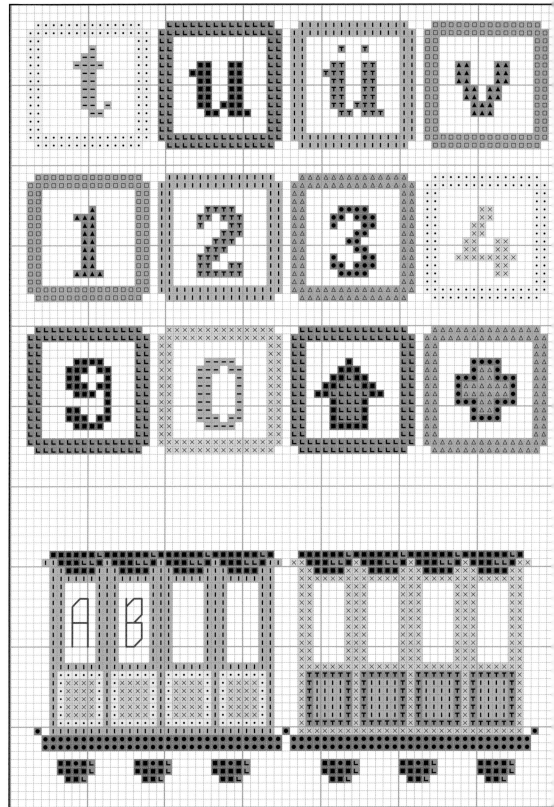

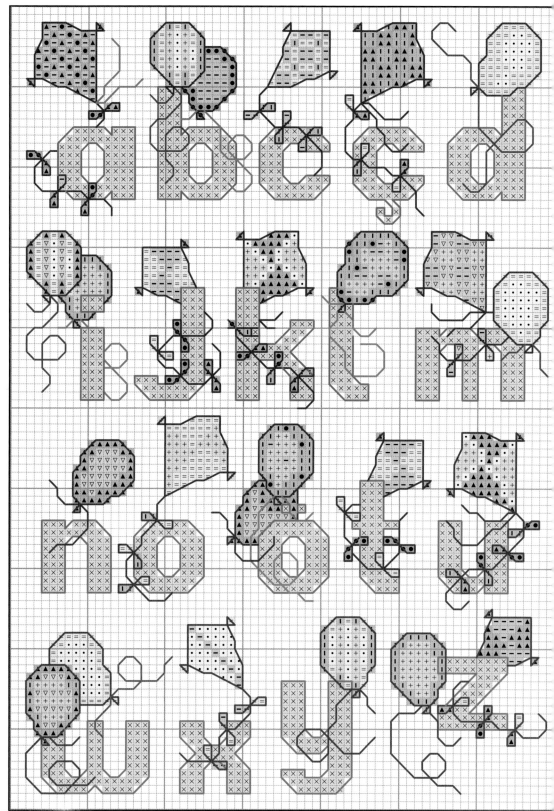

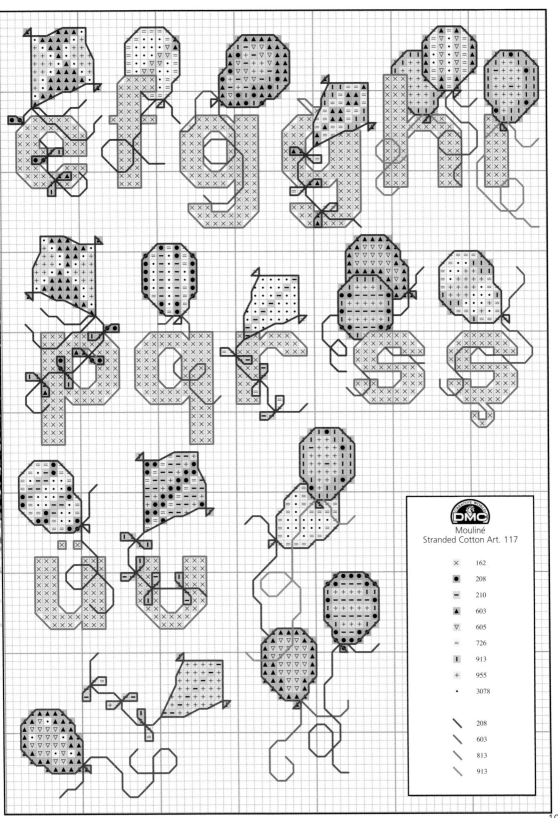

DMC
Mouliné
Stranded Cotton Art. 117

×	162
●	208
−	210
▲	603
▽	605
=	726
I	913
+	955
•	3078
╲	208
╲	603
╲	813
╲	913

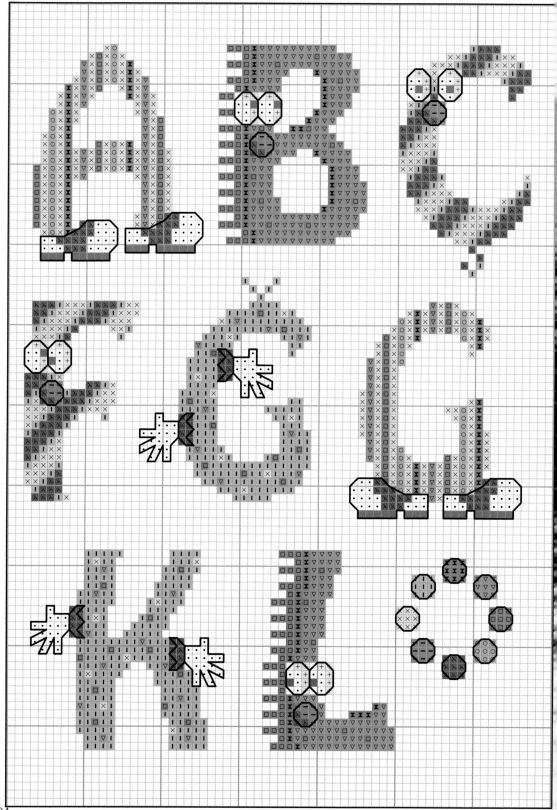

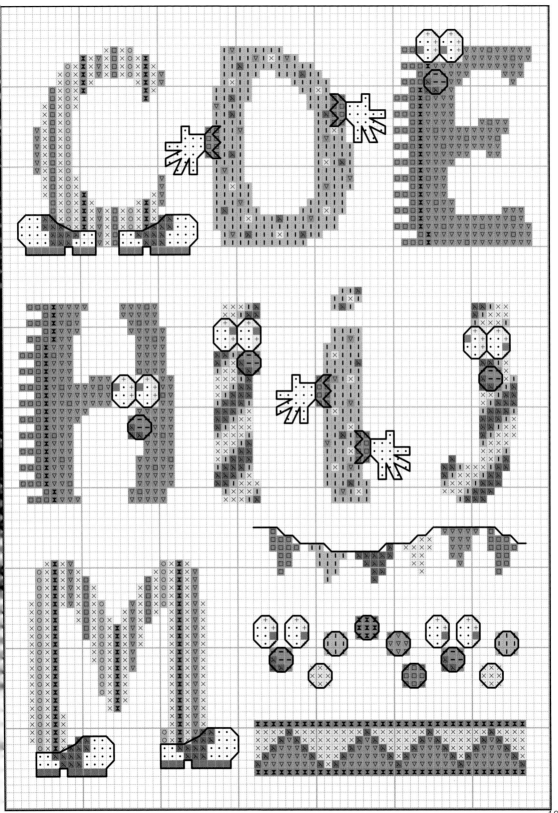

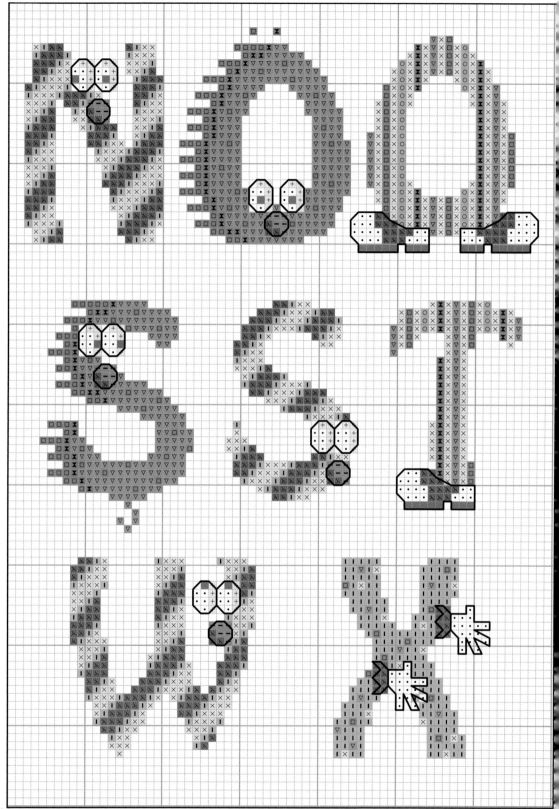

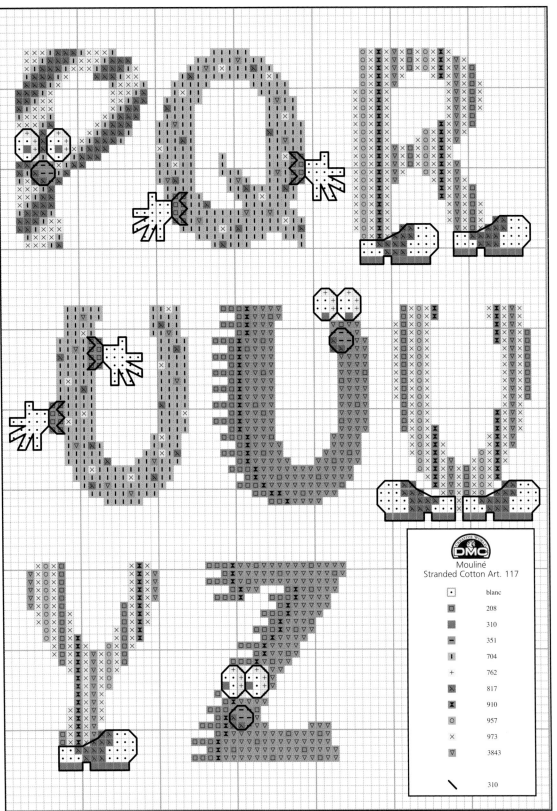

Mouliné
Stranded Cotton Art. 117

·	blanc
▢	208
▬	310
—	351
I	704
+	762
⊠	817
✕	910
○	957
✕	973
▽	3843
╲	310

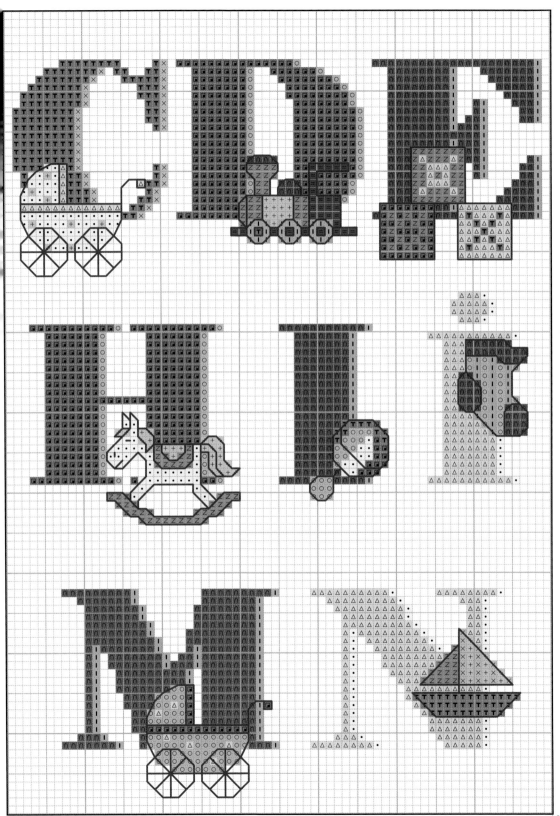

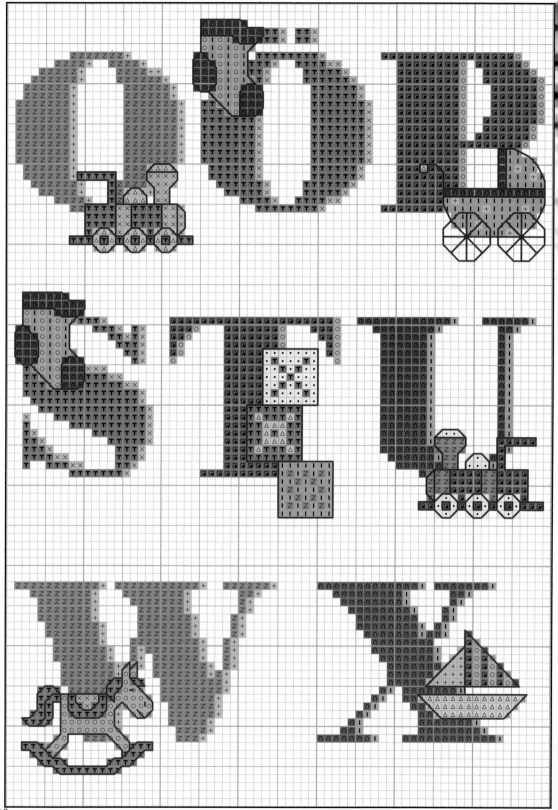

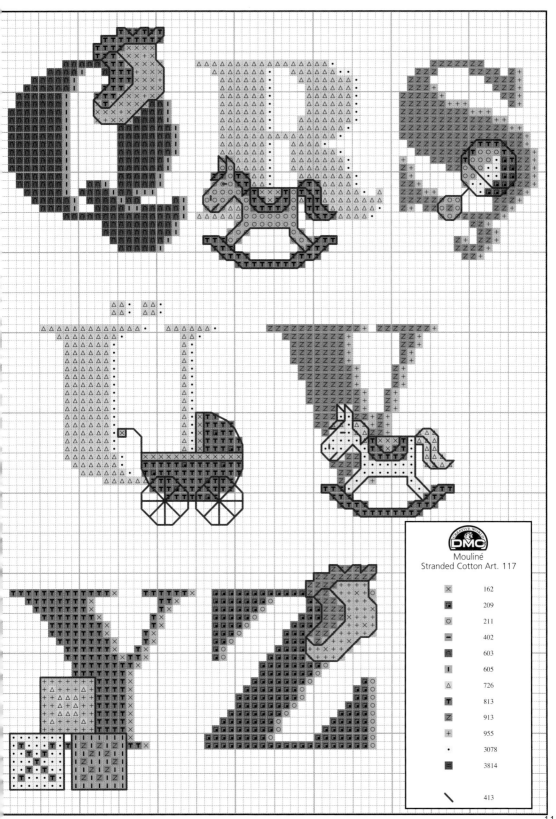

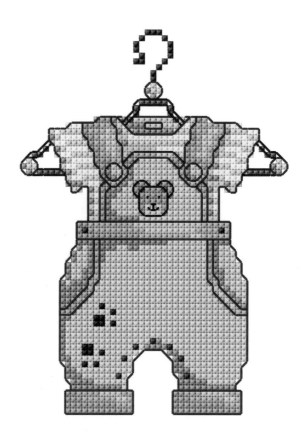